"The works of John Brown of Haddington, the orphaned shepherd boy who rose to become a revered pastor, theologian, and reformer, are a largely unmined treasure trove. I am therefore very grateful for Gregory Soderberg's new edition of Brown's carefully reasoned and pastorally practical treatise on the ordinary means of grace God affords us at the Lord's Table. This is a vital resource and, if possible, more relevant today than when it was written more than two centuries ago."

—GEORGE GRANT, PASTOR EMERITUS, PARISH PRESBYTERIAN CHURCH, AND DIRECTOR, KING'S MEADOW STUDY CENTER

"I am delighted to see this significant work by John Brown of Haddington available once again with the valuable historical introduction by Dr. Soderberg. More frequent communion, thoughtfully led, would enhance the health of our churches, and this brief address argues well for the practice. I hope it may stir many to consider more frequent communion."

—RAY VAN NESTE, PROFESSOR OF BIBLICAL STUDIES, UNION UNIVERSITY

"Dr. Soderberg puts us greatly in his debt by republishing for a contemporary audience John Brown of Haddington's apology for a more frequent celebration of Holy Supper. Having previously explored the post-Reformation debates on communion frequency on both sides of the Atlantic, Soderberg now helps us to see the present-day relevance of one of the most extraordinary sources he came across in his doctoral work. It is my hope that this 18th century treatise will help all those with an interest in the issue of communion frequency to make up their minds in a more well-considered way, and where appropriate make decisions that will strengthen and deepen the faith of their communities."

—GIJSBERT VAN DEN BRINK, PROFESSOR OF THEOLOGY & SCIENCE, VRIJE UNIVERSITEIT, AMSTERDAM

John Brown of Haddington on Frequent Communion

John Brown of Haddington on Frequent Communion

EDITED BY
GREGORY SODERBERG

WIPF & STOCK · Eugene, Oregon

JOHN BROWN OF HADDINGTON ON FREQUENT COMMUNION

Copyright © 2024 Gregory Soderberg. All rights reserved. Except for brief quotations in critical publications or reviews, no part of this book may be reproduced in any manner without prior written permission from the publisher. Write: Permissions, Wipf and Stock Publishers, 199 W. 8th Ave., Suite 3, Eugene, OR 97401.

Wipf & Stock
An Imprint of Wipf and Stock Publishers
199 W. 8th Ave., Suite 3
Eugene, OR 97401

www.wipfandstock.com

PAPERBACK ISBN: 979-8-3852-2862-1
HARDCOVER ISBN: 979-8-3852-2863-8
EBOOK ISBN: 979-8-3852-2864-5

11/18/24

Contents

Historical Introduction | vii

Preface | xv

An Apology, &c. | 1

Bibliography | 39

Historical Introduction

JOHN BROWN OF HADDINGTON's life is the stuff of legend. Rising from poverty, this orphaned child grew into one of Scotland's most respected and beloved preachers and authors. His inauspicious beginnings and his rapid acquisition of languages such as Latin and Greek prompted urban legends and spiteful slander. As a result, any summary of John Brown's life must navigate through a tantalizing mix of historical truth and hagiographical embellishment.

He was born in 1722, near Abernathy, in Scotland. An early experience of seeing the Lord's Supper administered and hearing the pastor preach movingly about Christ made a deep impression on him. His parents died when he was eleven, and he lived with various families. While tending sheep for an elderly man, John managed to teach himself Greek, Latin, and Hebrew. This was viewed with suspicion, and some even accused him of being taught by the devil. Brown eventually received ministerial training in the new seminary started by members of the Associate Synod of the Scottish Reformed church. After his ordination, he served as the minister in Haddington for thirty-six years, until his death in 1787. During those years, he taught numerous ministerial students for the Associate Synod and wrote several popular books. His catechism was especially popular in Presbyterian households in Northern Ireland.[1]

Brown's *Apology* was one of the main sources that I examined in my PhD dissertation. In my study I produced the first scholarly treatment of communion frequency polemics and practices in Reformed churches, focusing on the debates about communion frequency that engaged Scottish writers in the 1700–1800s. There, I summarized Brown's *Apology*:

> His *An Apology for the More Frequent Administration of the Lord's Supper* was published posthumously in 1804.[2] It is one of the more lucid treatments of communion frequency, containing many counter-arguments original to Brown.[3] According to the publisher's preface, Brown was the first minister in his association of churches to introduce bi-annual communion, though he desired greater frequency. The *Apology* was found in Brown's papers after his death, apparently edited and ready for publication. Although his pamphlet was published in 1804, Brown deals with many of the same themes as other Scottish pastors and theologians who also argued for greater communion frequency. Interestingly, he does not quote any of the other authors who were part of the Scots-Reformed communion frequency debates.

---

1. Macleod, *Scottish Theology*, 193.

2. For a brief biography, see Robertson, "John Brown of Haddington." See also W. Brown, *Life of John Brown*; Mackenzie, *John Brown of Haddington*; Macleod, *Scottish Theology*, 192–94.

3. Interestingly, Brown does not address the issue of communion frequency in his popular work of systematic theology, *Compendium View of Natural and Revealed Religion*, republished as *The Systematic Theology of John Brown of Haddington*.

Sections 1–7 deal with New Testament texts and church history, sections 8–11 present theological arguments, and section 11 answers objections. This last section is especially helpful, because the objections Brown considers provide insight into the common concerns about frequent communion at that time.[4]

John Brown of Haddington was the quintessential pastor-scholar. As a self-made man, an orphan who rose from poverty, perhaps this helped him to remain connected to his parishioners and their concerns. He always had time to write letters of encouragement to those struggling or grieving. He was intimately involved in the work of his denomination and was the main teacher for the church-based training program that produced pastors for the Secession, or Associate Synod, churches.

The sacrament of the Lord's Supper was central in Brown's conversion and in his ministry. As a child he attended a large communion observance in the town of Abernathy. Robert Mackenzie, a biographer of Brown, describes the event. It provides a sense of what Scottish communion practices were like in Brown's time, which is doubly important because it forms the background of his *Apology*:

> In most of the parishes at that time there was only an annual celebration of this ordinance. Days were allotted to it. Thousands attended from far and near. Abernathy was a favourite centre. There they gathered on the green slope at the foot of the hill to the south of the village, sitting in plaids on the green grass, the preacher standing in an elevated narrow shelter, like a sentry box. Within the church, the Communion

4. Soderberg, *As Often as You Eat*, 224–25.

proper proceeded, where those who were admitted who were privileged to sit down at the table. In turn the groups of communicants took their places at the reserved seats, reverently covered with white linen, while preacher after preacher addressed them, and distributed the sacred symbols. It was a profoundly impressive occasion.[5]

John Brown relates how the experience moved him in his *Memoir*:

> About the eighth year of my age, I happened in the crowd to get into the church on the sacrament Sabbath, when it was common for all but intended communicants to be excluded. The table or tables which I heard served before I was shut out, were chiefly served upon Christ, and in a sweet and delightful manner. This captivated my young affections, and has made me since think that little ones should never be excluded from the church on such occasions. Though what they may hear may not convert them, it may be of use to begin the allurement of their hearts to the Saviour.[6]

This experience of being drawn to the beauty of the Lord's Supper, and yet being excluded, drove Brown to institute changes in his own church's communion practices. According to Mackenzie, "In later years, he instituted a reform in the Communion Services of the Church, by the admission of young persons as witnesses of the celebration, and by a more frequent observance of the supper."[7]

Like many Scottish Reformed Presbyterians of his time, the sacrament of the Lord's Supper was central to

5. Mackenzie, *John Brown of Haddington*, 15.
6. W. Brown, *Life of John Brown*, 8.
7. Mackenzie, *John Brown of Haddington*, 15.

Brown's spiritual growth and development. In early adulthood, he relates that "meanwhile, the Lord, by powerful and pleasant impressions of his Word on my heart, particularly at sacramental occasions at Dunfermline, Burntisland, Falkirk, and Glasgow, marvellously refreshed my soul, and made these years perhaps the most pleasant that ever I had, or will have on earth. Discourses on these texts,— Heb. x. 37; Ezek. xxxvii. 12; Psalm xci. 2; and a Meditation on Psalm v. 7, were particularly ravishing."[8] Note here the combination of both the preached word of God and the visible words of God in the sacrament. For Protestants, the Lord's Supper must always be accompanied by the preaching of the word. But, particularly for the Scots Reformed, word and sacrament together often became a profoundly moving and transformational event.[9]

According to the publisher's note at the beginning of his *Apology* (reprinted here as the preface), in his ministry Brown took steps to introduce more frequent communion in his church but was unable to move the congregation to what he believed was the biblical and historical ideal for communion frequency: "He much regretted the unfrequent administration of the Lord's Supper, and did what was in his power to correct the abuse. He was the first who introduced the dispensation of it in the Secession twice a-year; before, it was only annual. Farther he found it impracticable to carry it."

The *Apology* was written at the end of his life and demonstrates his settled convictions after years of serious scholarship and practical pastoral labor, not the flights of fancy of a young and idealistic innovator. This is important to note when so many Evangelicals and even Reformed

---

8. W. Brown, *Life of John Brown*, 16.
9. See Billings, *Remembrance, Communion, and Hope*, esp. 45–56.

Protestants are drawn to more frequent communion, along with naïve conceptions about the "early church" or the beauty of liturgical worship.[10] Brown was a strong proponent of Scottish Reformed Calvinism *and* he also believed that more frequent communion was vital for the spiritual health of individual Christians and for the church.

Why is Brown relevant today? As I tell my students: *We study and learn from the past so we can live wisely in the present.* Reading Brown and the other Scottish writers who wrote about the issue of communion frequency helps us to realize the background and context of many church practices that we might take for granted. How often a church observes communion is often a matter of tradition, and an unexamined tradition at that. Brown presents his own reading of history and offers explanations of how the traditions of infrequent communion developed in church history. We do not have to accept all the details of his analysis to appreciate the intent. Throughout church history, matters of worship, liturgy, and communion practice were rarely the result of a committee meeting to examine the evidence on both sides and then present a consensus. Worship and communion frequency were certainly informed by the Scriptures, but they were also influenced by a host of other political, practical, and even economic factors.

The Reformation was inspired by a vision of determining all things, and especially worship, by the word of God. Accordingly, while Brown does deal with history, and does appeal to other theologians, he is concerned to present a biblical case for more frequent communion. Reading Brown and other Scots Reformed authors who advocated more frequent communion like John Erskine, Thomas

---

10. For more on this phenomenon, along with a helpful historical treatment of many of the issues involved, see Stewart, *In Search of Ancient Roots*.

Randall, and John Mitchell Mason (as well as those arguing for the status quo of infrequent communion in Scotland) helps us to see the best arguments on both sides of the issue. It also shows how different perspectives deal with the same facts of church history and the same biblical texts. We all have a bias, and reading authors from the past can help us to break out of the prison of the present.[11]

This short essay by a giant of the Scottish Reformed church is republished in the hopes that it may inspire another generation of pastor scholars to courageously confront the challenges of their own times, and to not accept anything simply because of the weight of tradition. As Brown did, may they examine their own beliefs and practices according to the word of God, learning from the past and living wisely in the present.

---

11. See the classic essay of C. S. Lewis on this topic, "On the Reading of Old Books" (*God in the Dock*, 200–207).

An

Apology

For The More

Frequent Administration

of the

Lord's Supper;

With

Answers to the Objections Urged

Against It.

By The Rev. John Brown,

Late Minister of the Gospel at Haddington, And

Professor of Divinity Under the Associate

(Burgher) Synod.

He being dead, yet speaketh.

EDINBURGH:

PRINTED BY J. RITCHIE.

FOR OGLE & AIKMAN, EDINBURGH; M. OGLE, GLASGOW;

AND R. OGLE, LONDON.

1804.

Preface

THE WRITER OF THE *following Apology is well known to the religious Public. He was long a respectable member of the Associate Church, and filled the Chair of Professor of Divinity with universal approbation. As a Scholar and Divine he had few equals. The numerous editions of several of his Works, are the best proof of the estimation in which he is held as an Author. He left two copies of the following Apology among his papers; one of which appears to have been corrected for publication. He much regretted the unfrequent administration of the Lord's Supper, and did what was in his power to correct the abuse. He was the first who introduced the dispensation of it in the Secession twice a-year; before, it was only annual. Farther he found it impracticable to carry it. But the time is now come when a greater reformation might be effected. In several places it is already begun, and it is hoped that it will soon be universal. Reader, throw prejudice aside, read with candour, and act according to your convictions.*

An
APOLOGY, &c.

CUSTOM OFTEN AUTHORIZES PRACTICES and principles so much, that one is sometimes ready to lay down even life itself in defense of them; but it certainly becomes every Christian to examine the most general and inveterate customs by reason and revelation, and to reject or receive the same, according as they abide the test or not.[1] On this footing, I here presume to call to the bar the practice of administering the sacrament of the Lord's supper so seldom, and am persuaded, that the more frequent administration of this ordinance should take place. My reasons are the following:[2]

1. Spelling has been modernized and Americanized, although some of the original formatting has been retained. In the 1700s and early 1800s, English typesetters routinely used *f* for many instances of *s*. In a few places, the language has been updated to more contemporary English. Headings have sometimes been added in brackets and/or placed in italics to help the reader track the flow of Brown's argumentation.

2. Here Brown follows a typical pattern among those arguing for more frequent communion in this time period: (1) biblical arguments, (2) arguments from church history, (3) opinions of Protestant theologians, (4) specific examples of Protestant confessions and church practices. See Soderberg, *As Often as You Eat*, 232–47, for a comparison of Brown and other Scottish writers and the arguments

I. [*New Testament Practice*] In the apostolic times it was ordinarily administered every Sabbath, as is granted by all those who have inquired into the history of these times.[3] This frequency has the approbation of the apostle Paul, 1 Cor 2:25–26, "This do ye, as oft as ye drink it, in remembrance of me. For as often as ye eat this bread, and drink this cup, ye do shew the Lord's death until he come." Here he expresses himself in such a manner as plainly approves of the accustomed frequency of the administration of this ordinance. Things peculiar to the apostolic age, were all such as tended to the founding of churches. But the sacrament of the supper has no connection with the founding, but with the building up and strengthening of churches. Have Christians no less need of this ordinance? Is Christ now less able or willing to supply their need? Or, has he transferred the virtue and usefulness of this ordinance to another? If none of these can be pretended, why count the example of the apostles a sufficient warrant for the observation of the first day Sabbath, for public worship, for holding synods and presbyteries, if we count not their example in the frequent administration of the supper also worthy of, and fit for our imitation?

II. [*Church History*] That the sacrament of the Lord's supper was generally administered every Lord's day, for the space of about three hundred years, is beyond dispute.[4]

---

typically used in arguing about the issue of communion frequency in the 1700–1800s.

3. Brown refers in a footnote to Luke 24:30, 31, 35; Acts 2:41, 46; 20:7; 2 Cor. 11:20, 21. He also refers to the authors Pliny, Justin Martyr, and Chrysostom, without specifying individual works.

4. Brown's footnote reads: "Vide [see] Justin Martyr, Tertullian, Augustine, Minutius Felix, Cyprian, Fortunatus, Basil, Ambrose, Jerome, and others of the ancient fathers, who either expressly state the fact, or allude to it."

If this practice was sinful, how is it that no witness was ever raised up to oppose it as a profanation of the ordinance? If it was duty, why follow we not the footsteps of the flocks, and ask for the good old way that we may walk therein?

III. All the *Protestant Divines* that I have read on this point, declare themselves zealous for the more frequent administration of this ordinance. Calvin in his *Institutes* says, "It ought to be administered every Lord's day, and the custom of communicating once a-year, has been introduced by the wiles of the devil."[5] Dr. Owen says, "It is to be administered every first day of the week, or at least as frequently as opportunity and conveniency can be obtained."[6] Luther, in preface to *Cat.*, says, "He does not deserve the name of a Christian, that can content himself with communicating less than three or four times a year."[7] I pass over Doolittle, Campbell, Willison, Henry,[8] and a multitude of others, because I can add,

IV. All the *Protestant churches* have opposed the administration of the sacrament of the supper only once or twice a-year, as a Popish corruption; and have appointed a

5. The relevant quote can be found in Calvin, *Institutes*. Calvin discusses communion frequency in general in 4.17.43–46.

6. Brown is referring to John Owen's *A Brief Instruction in the Worship of God and Discipline of the Churches of the New Testament* (1667), which is in the form of a catechism (Owen, *Works*, 15:512). See also Mayor, *Lord's Supper*, 111–13; Gribben, *John Owen*, 240. Jon D. Payne cites the *Brief Instruction* in his *John Owen*, 48n1. Payne collects twenty-five sermons from Owen on the Lord's Supper, along with a summary and analysis. All of this material is summarized in Soderberg, *As Often as You Eat*, 104–5.

7. Brown quotes here from the preface to Martin Luther's *Small Catechism* (1529), which can be accessed at https://bookofconcord. org/small-catechism/.

8. I survey Thomas Doolittle (1630?–1707), John Willison (1680–1750), and Matthew Henry (1662–1714) in Soderberg, *As Often as You Eat*. It is unclear to which "Campbell" Brown refers here.

more frequent administration of it, as soon as they shook off the yoke of Antichrist. Thus, at the Reformation, the church of Geneva appointed it to be administered twelve times in the year; the church of Scotland, in her first book of discipline, four times a-year; the church of France, at least four times; and resolve to appoint a more frequent dispensation of it, as soon as convenient; the church of Holland, six times; nay, the lowest I find upon this point is the church of England, which is well known to be behind most of the Protestant churches in many things—she appointed it only thrice in the year. If these churches, then, when the darkness and ignorance of people were not yet dispelled by the light of the purity of the gospel, appointed so frequent an administration of this ordinance, have not we reason to believe they would have administered it still more frequently, had the spirit of reformation continued with them, till they, by painful instruction, had more fully banished ignorance from the people?

It ought not to be objected, that all these acts were not always put into practice, for, it is certain, men's sentiments are better known from their declarations and decisions than from their practice. It is easier to decide and to declare, than to practice. Many neglected to administer the supper from very trifling reasons: some from sloth; and others from want of a fund to defray the charges; as if He, whose is the silver and the gold, could not have provided a single penny for every communicant, one with another, to purchase bread and wine to represent the body and blood of his beloved Son, in an ordinance so dear to him.

V. [*Reasons for Infrequent Communion in Church History*] The means by which the unfrequent administration of this ordinance appears to me to have been introduced into the church, do not savor of the God of truth.

The causes that occasioned its introduction appear to have been pride, superstition, covetousness, and carnal complaisance. The eastern hermits, retiring from the society of men, had taken up their residence in deserts and mountains, and being far removed from the places of its administration, seldom attended. This, though really the effect of their sloth and distance, they pretended to arise from their regard and reverence for this most solemn ordinance. It being easy to imitate them in this imaginary holiness, which lay in neglecting the ordinance of God, many of the eastern Christians left off to communicate, except at such times as superstition had rendered solemn, as at pasch[9]; and contented themselves with being spectators on other occasions. On account of this practice, we find the great and eloquent Chrysostom, once and again, bitterly exclaiming against them as guilty of the highest contempt of God and Christ; and calls their practice a most wicked custom.[10] A custom of sending part of the consecrated

9. "Pasch" refers to the ancient Greek name for Easter. Early in the history of the church, it became standard practice to baptize new believers at Pascha/Easter. It was viewed as the most important day of the Christian calendar. See "Easter," in Bradshaw, *New Westminster Dictionary*, 160–61.

10. One statement of John Chrysostom (347–407) on communion frequency originates in his third homily on Ephesians. There, he stridently rebukes his hearers for their failure to receive communion: "In vain is the daily Sacrifice, in vain do we stand before the Altar; there is no one to partake" (Chrysostom, *Homilies on Ephesians*, 13:64). In the context of the homily, Chrysostom is exhorting his congregation to repent of their sins and receive the Eucharist. Instead, many were apparently attending the rest of the church service, including the Eucharistic portion, although they did not receive communion. Chrysostom urges them: "That I may not then be the means of increasing your condemnation, I entreat you, not to forbear coming, but to render yourselves worthy both of being present, and of approaching" (13:64–65). Chrysostom is a good example of the theme of stressing the high standards of purity that qualify someone

elements to the absent, that they might partake of them in their own houses, now also taking place, frequently one or two of a family or village having joined in the public administration, carried off so much of the elements as might be divided among those who stayed behind, or reserved it for their own use afterward. This odd way of communicating being no way painful or expensive, many of the people were abundantly fond of it, and the number of communicants became by these means very small.

Further, the Christian people having got the supreme magistrate upon their side, thought themselves now more secure in the possession of their worldly wealth, and, therefore, were so much the more loath to part with it, in giving offerings every Sabbath. On these offerings the primitive ministers lived, and out of them the elements were taken; and, as it was discreditable then to partake without offering, except the person were known to be very poor, too many chose rather, for the most part of the year, to abstain from the sacramental table, than part with a little of their beloved substance. If the people were churlish, the priests were equally covetous. Though they now began to have other funds assigned them for their subsistence, they were far from willing to part with the ancient offerings; therefore, when they saw it was not possible to cause the people bring [sic] them every Sabbath, they reduced the frequency of the administration of the supper, in expectation that the people would attend better, and bring larger

---

to receive communion. His preaching also demonstrates the perennial struggle of motivating some people to come to the Eucharist. It is a theme and a tension evident in most other Christian traditions and denominations (Lutheran: Wieting, *Blessings of Weekly Communion*; Roman Catholic: Dougherty, *From Altar-Throne to Table*; Orthodox: Schmemann, *Eucharist*, 242–45; and Taft, "Frequency of the Eucharist," 93).

offerings. And in order to inflame them the more powerfully to do this, the clergy fixed the administration to times now consecrated by superstition, and began, by little and little, to persuade the people that their offerings were meritorious, and were a proper sacrifice for the atonement of their sins. Hence sprung at last that notion, that so much as was consecrated was turned into Christ's real body and blood, and was, as such, offered by the priests to atone for the sins of the quick and the dead.

Besides, when the Christian church began to share the smiles and support of the emperor and his court, multitudes, influenced by carnal motives, thronged into it, and the reins of discipline being now relaxed, they were easily admitted, though indeed many of them were far from being visible saints. These carnal and court Christians disliked being from week to week employed in self-examination, and other preparatory work, or living under the impression of so frequent solemn approaching to God.[11] They

11. In the fourth century, when the church became respectable and the church enjoyed the official patronage of the political rulers, there was a noticeable tendency towards laxity. The fires of persecution died out, and it became easier to be a nominal Christian. In reaction to this, preachers like John Chrysostom and others "tried to exhort their congregations to amend their lives and come worthily to receive the sacrament, but this had the opposite effect from that intended: many people then preferred to come to church and not receive communion rather than undertake the moral reformation asked of them in order to be communicants. This increased the tendency that was already forming for the eucharist to be viewed as something done by the clergy for the people rather than, as before, an action of the whole people of God. For those who now began to receive communion only infrequently, the eucharist not only ceased to be a communal action but was not even seen as food to be eaten. Instead, it became principally an object of devotion, to be gazed on. It is not surprising, therefore, that ancient liturgical commentators then began to interpret the rite in terms of a drama that unfolded before the eyes of the spectators" ("Eucharist," in Bradshaw, *New*

also disliked the simplicity of this, as well as of other gospel ordinances, and were mightily fond that the Christian worship should be modelled as near to the Pagan and Jewish forms as possible. The clergy, possessed with the same vitiated taste, and, besides, being very solicitous to procure themselves the favor of the great, transformed the Christian worship according to these patterns; and as the Pagans had in the year only a few solemn feasts to honor of their gods, and the Jews had only three solemn feasts, the feast of the Passover at Easter, the feast of Harvest at Pentecost, and the feast of Tabernacles, they appointed the supper to be administered to the people at Christmas, to supply the place of the feast of the Bacchanals, and at Easter and Pentecost, to supply the place of two of the Jewish feasts. However, this conforming of Christ's ordinance (as now indeed is also the case) did not procure due attendance on it, and therefore the clergy afterwards reduced the administration of it to the people to once, namely Easter.

By these means, and in this manner, it appears to me, from the hints of the history of these times which I can come to the knowledge of, was the unfrequency of the administration of the Lord's supper chiefly introduced. The clergy, however, pretended regard to the solemnity of the ordinance as the reason of all these alterations; and I doubt not but some good men were blinded, as to imagine that their conduct had a real tendency to produce this effect.

VI. [*Reasons for Infrequent Communion in Church History, Pt. 2*]. As often as the church of Christ has been in a flourishing state, greater frequency has been practiced or pursued. Thus it was in the primitive ages; thus it was at the Reformation; thus it was in that glorious assembly of the church of Scotland, 1638, thus also the Westminster

---

Westminster, 172–73).

AN APOLOGY, &C.

Assembly of Divines declare in their Directory, that it should be frequently administered. While things went in some measure well after the Revolution, sundry acts were passed to encourage and press the more frequent administration of it; and the Assembly appointed presbyteries to order the administration of it, so that people may have opportunity to communicate every month of the year.

On the other hand, a declension towards the unfrequent celebration of this ordinance, has been generally the close attendant of apostasy and backsliding. Thus, under Popery, the administration was reduced from once every week, to three times, and afterwards to once a year; and however much this last was practiced, yet it was never authorized till Popery had arrived at a prodigious height. The same monster of a Pope, and dupe of a council did, AD 1215, first ratify the doctrine of Transubstantiation, and then pass an act, allowing the administration of the supper to the people, and their partaking of it once a year, to be sufficient; though even that act intimates, that it is lawful to do it oftener.[12]

---

12. Brown refers here to the Fourth Lateran Council (1215) and Pope Innocent III (1160/61–1216), who expanded the political and secular power of the papacy. The Fourth Lateran Council, the council that condemned Jan Hus to the stake, mandated an annual reception of the Eucharist. The beginning of canon 21 reads: "All the faithful of either sex, after they have reached the age of discernment, should individually confess all their sins in a faithful manner to their own priest at least once a year, and let them take care to do what they can to perform the penance imposed on them. Let them reverently receive the sacrament of the eucharist at least at Easter unless they think, for a good reason and on the advice of their own priest, that they should abstain from receiving for a time. Otherwise they shall be barred from entering a church during their lifetime and they shall be denied a christian [sic] burial at death" (Tanner, *Decrees of the Ecumenical Councils*, 1:245).

In the first period of Episcopacy in Scotland, the administration of the supper was reduced from twice or four times a-year to once, namely, at Easter. Thus also in the second period of Episcopacy, though in the period before the ministers had pushed, some or all of them practiced a more frequent administration, the perjured bishops and curates reduced it to once a-year; and had not Easter been the child of superstition, it is likely it would have been still more unfrequent.[13]

In the present period of apostasy, have we not known this ordinance neglected two, three, or even seven years together, by some ministers?[14] And would it not be more so, if fear of being forced to refund what they yearly receive for communion elements, did not influence many ministers more than their consciences do?

VII. [*Reasons for Infrequent Communion in Church History, Pt. 3*]. God's witnesses for truth in backsliding periods, have been wont to bear witness in favor of the more frequent administration of this ordinance. Thus these men of God, Chrysostom, Ambrose, Augustine, &c. exclaim bitterly against the reduction of it to a few times in the year;

---

13. Here, Brown refers to the period of Charles II (1660–85), who tried to reimpose Episcopalian church government and worship in England, Scotland, and Wales with the Act of Uniformity in 1662. Many hundreds of ministers throughout Britain refused to comply and lost their parishes in what became known as the "Great Ejection." So, Brown's phrase "minsters had pushed" most likely hearkens back to this event. They were either pushed out of their jobs by the act or they pushed away themselves, as a boat pushing away from shore. For more on the historical context, especially as it relates to the observance of communion, see Spurr, *Post-Reformation*, 144–54; Burnet, *Holy Communion*, 135–47.

14. On infrequent communion in the Scottish Reformed tradition and the many factors that contributed to patterns of communion observance, see Soderberg, *As Often as You Eat*, 136–45; Burnet, *Holy Communion*, ch. 7.

and when things were yet worse, as to the unfrequency of it, in the ninth century, Bertram and Rabanus, the two most learned and upright men of the age, testified against it, and insisted that the custom of their times should be corrected by the primitive pattern.[15] About 1627, Messrs. Robert Blair and Cunningham agreed each to have it four times a-year. About 1630, these great men of God in Ireland who witnessed against Episcopacy, namely Messrs. John Livingstone, Robert Blair, Robert Cunningham, Josias Welsh, &c. administered this sacrament twice a year to their people, and were disposed to have done it oftener, had not nine or ten of them, being situated about twenty miles, concerted measures so as the bulk of their people communicated eighteen or twenty times in the year.[16]

VIII. [*Effects of Infrequent Communion*] The unfrequent administration of this ordinance, tends to encourage looseness in practice among professors. These are generally under some impressions of the awe and dread of God, when they are approaching to this ordinance, which, were it frequently repeated, might be deepened and increased; but, when they approach it so seldom, they, as Calvin says, receive it as a clearance of accounts with God, and so give up themselves to sloth and sin, till another sacramental occasion excites some fresh concern.[17]

---

15. "Bertram" is Ratramnus (d. 868), and "Rabanus" is Rabanus Maurus (c. 780–856).

16. Brown cites the example of Scottish Presbyterian ministers laboring in Ireland. Robert Blair (1593–1666), John Livingstone (1603–72), Robert Cunningham (d. 1637), and Josias Welsh (1598–1634), who was John Knox's grandson, were all Scottish ministers who labored to establish the Presbyterian movement in Northern Ireland. They were all also involved, in various ways, in the revivals that occurred in that region. For more on these movements, see Westerkamp, *Triumph of the Laity*; Schmidt, *Holy Fairs*.

17. It is not clear which writing of Calvin that Brown has in mind

Besides, ministers administering this ordinance unfrequently, tends to encourage people to partake of it seldom, as they see no more warrant for frequent participation, than for frequent administration.

IX. [*Benefits of Frequent Communion*] It cannot be denied that this ordinance is, of all others, the most calculated for communicating spiritual supplies of grace; for enabling the believer to defeat the devil and indwelling lusts, and to overcome the world in all its allurements; for intimating the love of Christ, and giving discoveries of him in his glory and blessings, and bringing him near unto the arms of faith; for sealing pardon, conveying comforts, clearing doubts, kindling, quickening, and strengthening love to Christ and his people. Have not believers then frequently need of it? And, if it should prove such an ordinance to them, as it will do if conscientiously managed, would it not be much to their advantage frequently to partake of it? What wonders of saints were the primitive Christians, who communicated every Sabbath! What wonders of saints were those in the north of Ireland in 1630, who communicated eighteen or twenty times a-year![18] What if the great want of love to the brethren, in comparison of what took place in the primitive times, be owing to our seldom partaking of this ordinance!

If the conscientious improvement of this ordinance tend so remarkably to the advantage of believers, ought they not frequently to partake of it? Ought they not, if possible, to go to the utmost extent of frequency that Christ allows? It will not be denied, that Christ allows conscientious communicating every Sabbath. Now, if Christ does so,

---

here.

18. Brown refers here to the revivals, centered on celebrations of the Lord's Supper, in Northern Ireland, during the ministries of John Livingstone et al.

shall men not allow it? Shall ministers, if possible, not order matters so, that believers may have opportunity to communicate conscientiously, as often as Christ allows them?

Again, if frequent communicating be commendable, frequent administration is so too; for in every congregation there are many who, by reason of service, weakness, poverty, etc., cannot travel to a sacrament at ten, twelve, twenty, thirty, or forty miles distance.[19] Servants cannot be allowed so many days as are necessary for going to, attending on, and returning from the ordinance, if it is dispensed at a distance. The weak cannot walk. The poor cannot afford the necessary expenses, especially when it is considered that, in many places, poor strangers are taken little notice of, even by those who are sufficiently able to take them in; from which it follows, that if persons have not the means of maintaining themselves, they must starve if they venture to come abroad to such occasions. Is it not the poor of the flock who especially wait upon Christ? Now, if their richer brethren by profession cruelly prevent their being able to communicate abroad, ought not ministers, if possible, to give them the opportunity at home?

---

19. Brown is referring to the custom of large "communion seasons," where multiple communities would gather to celebrate communion. Ministers from the different churches would preach in turn. The communion was typically preceded by a day of preaching devoted to helping people prepare for receiving communion. On the day of communion there would be another sermon before communion, and then shorter "table addresses" to each group that came successively to the table. Since the Scottish Reformed typically celebrated around an actual table, it could take much of the day for everyone in the large gathering to take turns communing at the table. On the Monday after a communion Sunday, there were still more sermons, called "Thanksgiving" sermons. These "communion fairs" (as they came to be known) were both social and spiritual events. See Soderberg, *As Often as You Eat*, 136–45; Schmidt, *Holy Fairs*; Westerkamp, *Triumph of the Laity*.

Is it not then merciless, is it not cruel, in an overseer of souls, to allow such persons but one or two sacramental meals in the year, when it lies in his power to afford them more? Christ allows them to communicate every Sabbath; Christ's servants voluntarily refuse to allow them to communicate above once or twice in the year, by keeping away the sacrament from their bounds![20]

X. [*Communion Frequency and Scottish Church History*] Every Seceding minister does, in his ordination vows and otherwise, solemnly approve the administration of the sacrament of the supper more frequently than is at present practiced, and, either more or less directly, promises to practice it if possible. Do not Seceding ministers, in their ordination vows, adhere to the Testimony? Yes, surely. Well, does not the Testimony expressly adhere to the first Book of Discipline, except in such things as were particularly calculated for the circumstances of that time in which it was written?[21] And, does not the first Book of Discipline appoint, that every minister celebrate the Lord's supper four times a year?[22] Now, can it be said that this is a matter

20. Brown displays a unique concern for servants and the poor, who were unable to journey to the large communion celebrations in Scotland. In many ways, Reformed theology that stressed the need to prepare spiritually for the supper privileged those who had the time to devote to such preparation. In effect, this could create a two-tiered system of spirituality.

21. The "Testimony" of 1737 is the statement of beliefs of the Associate Presbytery (also called the Associate Synod, or Seceders, or Secession), the group of churches within which Brown ministered. It includes statements justifying the synod's split from the established church of Scotland. For the background of the split and a summary of the content of the testimony, see Westerkamp, *Triumph of the Laity*, 112–20.

22. For the First Book of Discipline, other Scottish ecclesial statements, and their teachings on communion frequency, see Soderberg, *As Often as You Eat*, 81–87.

peculiarly calculated for the circumstances of that period? On the contrary, it is certain that the people were ignorant, and had little means of instruction; and will anybody say, that the more ignorant people are, they should have this sacrament administered the oftener to them?

Does not the same Testimony expressly declare our adherence to the Westminster Directory for Worship? Yes, it does. Well, does not that Directory expressly declare, that the Lord's supper ought to be frequently administered, though it leaves to the minister and elders to determine its frequency in their congregations? When it says, *frequently administered in their congregations*, will anybody say that its meaning is, "it ought to be once or twice a-year administered," though both minister and elders think it for edification that it should be done oftener?

Again, does not the Testimony expressly declare an adherence to all the Acts of Assembly between 1638 and 1650, and those since that time which are calculated for promoting reformation? And, are there not among these some that require the sacrament of the supper to be administered more frequently than is a present practiced?[23] Yes, there are. Now, do these promote reformation? If so, the Papists were mighty reformers in this point, especially in the thirteenth century, when about their worst; and all the Protestant churches have been a sect of apostates, and the apostles the principal ringleaders in the defection. Or say, do not these acts promote reformation, that is, a

23. It is unclear to which Acts of Assembly Brown is specifically referring. The Church of Scotland addressed the issue of multi-parish communion gatherings in 1645 without mentioning the issue of frequency explicitly. However, beginning in 1701, the General Assembly began to direct churches towards more frequent communion. See Soderberg, *As Often as You Eat*, 142–45. For the records of the General Assembly of the Church of Scotland from 1638 to 1842, see British History Online, "Acts of General Assembly."

conformity to the practice of the church before Popery had defiled her? Certainly, according to this plain explication of the word *reformation*, they do. Then, does it not necessarily follow, that they are approven and espoused in the Testimony?

XI. [*Arguments against Frequent Communion with Responses*] All the arguments I ever knew advanced in support of the unfrequent administration of the Lord's supper, appear to me altogether destitute of force. The following are the principal:

Objection I. The frequent administration of this ordinance, in the apostolic and primitive[24] ages of Christianity, was commendable and necessary, because the continual perfections that then raged gave them ground to fear every Sabbath might be their last; whereas now we are not in such danger, and therefore need not so frequent use of this ordinance.

Answer. Ought we not to still to live as if every Sabbath were to be our last? Have we now a lease of life more than these had? Did not many Christians in those times live to as great age as we now do? Indeed, is it not evident, from the best historians, that the church was generally under no persecution above one third part of the time that weekly communion was practiced? But say they had been constantly exposed to the cruelest persecution, the objection becomes still more absurd. If they attended this ordinance weekly at the peril of their lives, does it follow that now, when God gives us greater and better opportunity for it, we ought to omit it? Does God require the greatest work at his people's hands, when he gives least opportunity? Or, does he require least work when he gives the greatest

---

24. In this context, "primitive" was closer to "primal," in the sense of closer to an origin. See Soderberg, "Ancient Discipline and Pristine Doctrine."

opportunity for it? What kind of a master must God be if this were the case? Besides, do not men need this ordinance to preserve them from the influence of the world's smiles, as much as of its frowns? Whether, indeed, has the first or the last been ordinarily most hurtful to the souls of Christians? Is not then the need of this ordinance now greater than in the primitive ages? Did the apostles and others administer this sacrament so often, that persons, being daily in danger of death, might, if possible, have its sacred elements in their belly in their dying moments, as a Popish viaticum to ensure their soul's escape from hell and purgatory in that critical juncture?

[*Inverting the Objection*] Let us invert this objection, and try if it has not more force. It would then run thus: The primitive Christians received the Lord's supper weekly, as their souls were in greater danger from the smiles and allurements of the world, which are usually found more hurtful to men's spiritual concerns than its frowns; and as they had greater opportunity for doing so by their enjoying peace and liberty yet this frequency of administering and partaking is not requisite now, as we, being under the world's frowns, are in less hazard as to our spiritual concerns; and especially, as we cannot attend upon it but at the peril of our lives, God having expressly declared, that he loves mercy better than sacrifice.

Objection II. The primitive and reforming times were seasons of great spiritual liveliness, and of large communications of divine influences to the souls of believers; whereas it is quite otherwise now. Therefore, though frequent administration was then commendable, yet, in our languishing decayed state it is unnecessary.

Answer. Ought we to repair seldom to the wells of salvation, because we can bring but little water at once from them? Ought we seldom to endeavor to fill our pitchers at the fountain of living waters, because they are small? Is not this ordinance a cordial for restoring the languishing, strengthening the weak, recovering the sick, and reviving the dying believer? How reasonable, then, is it to argue that languishing, weak, sick, and dying believers, must not have it often administered to them, just because they are not in perfect health? Ought the weak and sickly child to be seldom allowed suck, just because it is not healthy and strong? Ought a weak, sick, languishing person, to be refused the frequent use of cordials and physic, for this very reason, that he has not a strong, robust, healthful condition? If a garden which, while often watered, continued moist and fruitful, become dry, withered, and barren, when watered only once a-year, ought it to be seldom watered, just because it is dry and withered? If it is not a duty to administer the supper frequently, when Christians are in a languishing decay, then it natively follows that they ought, for the same reason, seldom to communicate. Thus, because they are thirsty and parched, they must not drink; because they sit in darkness, they must beware of approaching near unto God, that he may be a light unto them, because they are oppressed with deadness, they must avoid using the means of revival.

[*Inverting the Objection*] Would not the objection inverted read better? The primitive Christians had this ordinance frequently administered to them, because, being decayed and withered, weak and sickly, and receiving only scanty communications of divine influence at once, it was necessary for them to be often taking new meals: Whereas we, being now strong and lively Christians, and receiving on sacramental occasions such large supplies of grace, as are sufficient to enable us to walk many days under their powerful influence, have no occasion for so frequently attending on that ordinance, which is especially calculated for strengthening languishing, weak, sickly believers.

Besides, are not the influences of the Spirit, spiritual strength, liveliness, and light, necessary to our right management of prayer, meditation, self-examination, reading, hearing, preaching, &c. as well as to a right observance of the Lord's supper? Would it not be as reasonable then to infer, from the present withdrawment of the Spirit, that we should seldom attend upon these ordinances, as once a month, or once a year, until the Spirit be poured from on high? Can anything be more absurd?

Objection III. If the Lord's supper were frequently administered, it would become less solemn, and, in time, quite contemptible, as we see in the case with baptism, through the frequency of the administration of that ordinance.

Answer. Is this mean [*sic*] of keeping up the credit of the Lord's supper of God's devising or not? If it is, where is that part of his word that warrants it? The contrary I have already proved from Scripture. Since, then, it is only of men's invention, what ground is there to hope it will really maintain the credit and solemnity of the ordinance? Did not the Papists of old pretend to maintain and advance its solemnity, by reduction of the frequency of administration? Did they not take away the cup from the people, which, Calvin says, was the native consequence of the former?[25] Did they not annex the administration of this ordinance to those seasons which superstition had aggrandized; namely, Easter, Pentecost, and Christmas? Did they not pretend that it was a real sacrifice, and that the elements were changed by consecration into the real body and blood of Christ?

---

25. Calvin makes this argument in *Institutes* 4.17.46–47.

And, did all this tend to the support of the proper credit of this ordinance? On the contrary, did it not destroy it? Though the doctrine of transubstantiation procured a kind of reverence for it, yet, was this reverence divine? Or, was it not rather devilish, in worshipping the elements? Now, how are we sure that our unfrequent administration of this ordinance will more effectually support its solemnity? Is it not strange that we should have so much encouragement from the practice of the apostles, the primitive Christians, and the whole of the reformed churches, to profane this solemn ordinance; while the most ignorant and abandoned Papists are our original pattern for the course that tends to support its proper honor and credit? What a strange case this must be, if, in order to support the credit of God's ordinance, we must forsake the footsteps of the flock, and walk in the paths originally chalked out by the most ignorant and wicked anti-Christians?[26]

Besides, if our unfrequent administration of this ordinance render it solemn, would it not become much more so, if administered only once in seven, ten, twenty, thirty, sixty, or an hundred years? If it is said, many might then die without receiving it, we reply, they may be saved notwithstanding; and may not many die, after their conversion, before they have an opportunity of partaking with us?

Further, it may be asked, why all this partiality for the honor of the sacrament of the supper? Why is not baptism also restricted to once or twice a-year? Why are we not taught that we should seldom pray, read, hear, and meditate, in order to keep up the solemnity of these ordinances, and to avoid the formality in them? Can any reason be

---

26. It was a common belief among Protestants at this time that the pope was the "antichrist" and that the entire Roman Catholic system of beliefs and practices was "anti-Christian" in this eschatological sense.

assigned, why unfrequency should preserve the honor of the Lord's supper, and not also preserve the honor and solemnity of these divine ordinances? Shall we not then find, that those who pray once a-month, or hear sermon once a-year, leave their minds far more religiously impressed with solemn views of God, than those who pray seven times a day, and hear a hundred sermons within the year? Shall we not find, that those who take care never to go out of their own congregation, to communicate in any other place, have far more deep and due impressions of this ordinance upon their spirits, than those who communicate ten or twelve times a-year? Shall we not find, that it will be a most wise course to have no sacraments during the whole winter season, as, by this long interval, persons are fitted for coming forward to it in the beginning of summer, with very solemn impressions of it upon their spirits? Shall we not find, that those who frequently communicate will approach unto God with less solemnity at the end of summer than at the beginning? And, if so, why do we not warn people against a practice that takes off a due impression of God from their minds? Is not this ordinance a means of eminent communion with God? Yes, it is. Is it not dispensed in order that Christ's friends may have eminent communion with God? Yes, surely. Now, does eminent communion with God, frequently obtained, make our impressions of God or his ordinances less solemn, and more contemptible? Yes, it certainly must. If frequent administration of the means of this communion render it more contemptible, frequent communion with God must render men formal in their addresses to him, if the objection have any force.

As to baptism, is it the frequent administration of this ordinance that renders it so contemptible? Then, why not reduce it to once a year? There is no more necessity of it to salvation than of the supper. Is it not rather the promiscuous administration of it to the children of ignorant and profane persons, together with the private administration of it, and the short cursory prayers in administering it, that are the true causes of the contempt under which it lies? Moreover, the annexing so many sermons and days to the administration of the Lord's supper, while baptism, a seal of the same covenant, where the same blessings are made over, the same Christ represented, and the same vows made, is administered as if it were a trifling ordinance, which does not come within many degrees of the solemnity of the other, causes many to look upon baptism as far inferior to the Lord's supper.

[*Inverting the Objection*] Let us invert this objection, and see how it stands. All human devices to render God's ordinances more solemn, are impeachments of his wisdom, and have always tended to bring the ordinances into contempt. But unfrequent administration of the supper is a human device, first invented by the worst of Papists, and therefore it tends to bring contempt on this ordinance, as we see sadly verified in the practice of those who voluntarily communicate seldom. Or thus, eminent communion with God, frequently enjoyed, is the most effectual means for impressing the mind with due reverence of him and his ordinances. Now, the Lord's supper is the ordinance in which the most remarkable communion with God is to be enjoyed; and therefore, as frequent use of this sacrament as Christ allows of, is the most eminent means for fixing a religious reverence of God, and of this, and of all other ordinances, upon the minds of believers.

Further, whether is it the frequent repetition of this ordinance upon the same spot of earth, in the same house;

or is it the repetition of it to the same people that prostitutes it? If the first, how do the dust and stones influence the contempt of it? If it is the second, then, certainly, it is a partial prostitution of it to administer it frequently to the same persons in different places. Does not this as much tend to render it contemptible, as if we had administered it an equal number of times in the same place, within the same time? If it is a prostitution to administer it frequently to them all, is it not likewise so to administer it to a part? Why then do we not exert ourselves to warn people against receiving the supper frequently, though at different places, since this is a great a prostitution of the ordinance, as to them, as if they received it frequently in the same spot?[27]

Objection IV. If people did communicate conscientiously, it would indeed fix deeper and more due impressions of God and his ordinances; and, in that case, though they had the sacrament administered to them every Sabbath, it would redound to their advantage; but when so much unworthy communicating already takes places when it is but seldom administered, there is little occasion to administer it oftener, as this would afford occasion for more unworthy communicating.

Answer. The whole of this objection is drawn from the abuse of the ordinance by unworthy communicating; but, if it have any force, might we not infer that it ought to be administered only once in twelve, twenty, a hundred, or even a thousand years, since even in this last case there would be too much unworthy communicating?

---

27. This was one argument on the side of those who argued for the status quo of infrequent communion (see "Objection V" below). They maintained that those who desired more frequent communion could travel to other towns where it was celebrated to receive it more often.

If the great abuse of an ordinance is a reason for omitting it, then farewell to all gospel ordinances, as none of them ever was, nor ever will be but greatly abused. Must we then pray, read, preach, hear, &c. but seldom, because all these ordinances are sadly abused? If the abuse of an ordinance is any reason against the frequent use of it, why preach we any more than one Sabbath in the year, since to many our preaching is the savor of death unto death, and gives men an occasion to trample underfoot the blood of the Son of God? Must God himself be impeached for giving Christ to be the Savior of the world, and for giving the world frequent offers of him, since he knew many would abuse him, by making this gift the occasion of their greater sin, and more dreaded ruin? Are not the air, the earth, and all the other gifts of God, daily abused? Ought he, therefore, to deprive all mankind of the use of them? Or, is he chargeable with the guilt of this abuse if he do not? According to the objection, he certainly is.

Indeed, might not ministers prevent much of the abuse that frequently takes place, in the case of the administration of the supper? Might they not conscientiously deny admission to all ignorant and scandalous persons? And, if they do, ought Christ's children to be starved, because the dogs will snatch at their food, or because they themselves cannot receive it as they ought? Say not, believers might be nourished by other gospel ordinances, though they wanted the more frequent use of this; for might they not be nourished by prayer, meditation, etc. without the preaching of the word? Might not the elect even be converted by reading God's word? Would it therefore be a small affair, nay a duty, to allow them only once a year the preaching of the word, an ordinance more especially appointed for that effect? Besides, whether do men involve themselves in most guilt by causing, or merely by occasioning the abuse? The decision of this point requires not a moment's hesitation. In the former case, a man joins issue with the devil; in the latter, he joins issue with God. Well, what if by reason of the long intervals between a believer's opportunities to draw near to God, and enjoy communion with him in this ordinance, their souls are rendered sadly carnal, and destitute of that humility, awe of God, and love to him and his people, which frequent nearness to him would have produced, and so they must come to this ordinance cold, like irons which have been long out of the fire, and, consequently, must greatly abuse it. Now, those ministers who withhold from believers the frequent use of this ordinance, have an active hand in all this coldness and deadness, which might have prevented, had not the intervals between opportunities of communicating been unnecessarily rendered so long. Well, ought ministers, merely in order to shun occasioning unworthy communicating, in which God joins with them, to involve themselves in negligently causing unworthy communicating, in which they join issue with Satan? Ought they, under pretense of preventing the guilt of some, to involve themselves and others in the very same guilt? Says not the apostle, that the damnation of such is just?

Objection V. Such as are willing may attend sacramental occasions in other congregations, and then multitudes of saints may meet, and, with their united prayers, draw down remarkable blessings on the ordinance. Many ministers will come up, whose various gifts will be more pleasing and edifying than if there were a few; and a fast, if not two, with a Friday exercise, three sermons on the Saturday, with two on the Monday, are all got through; by all which the proper dignity and solemnity of this ordinance is kept up, which could not be the case if it were frequently administered in each congregation.[28]

Answer. Can all that are dear to God attend sacramental occasions at the distance of ten, twenty, thirty, or forty miles? How shall servants, the weak, and the poor do so? What if two thirds of a congregation be of this sort? Shall ministers pity such least, when it is known Christ pitied them most?

Besides, might not as many meet on every occasion, though the sacrament were administered in the same place three or four times yearly, as do at present? If they are suitably profited by this ordinance, it is certain believers would be more desirous after fresh opportunities; and, what loss would there be, though some hypocrites stayed at home? Would not the force of prayers be three or four times as great than it is at present? Indeed, what if ministers *practically* encouraging frequent communion so little, by administering this ordinance seldom, be the reason why so few attend sacramental occasions in other places? Are not the people under the charge of these ministers that speak against the frequent ministration of this ordinance, among the most slothful and careless in this respect? Though believers have occasion to communicate in their own congregation four times a year, yet, if they can, does not Christ allow them to communicate other forty-eight times? Will, then, their communicating aright four times, influence them to be so far behind, if it is in their power to wait upon other opportunities? If pastors administer in their congregations as often as possible, can they not with a good grace excite their people to attend in other places, which they cannot

---

28. This objection refers to the multi-parish "communion fairs" that had become standard practice in Scottish Reformed churches in the 1700–1800s. See 13n19 above.

conscientiously do, if they neglect the administration of it when they might have the opportunity?

Indeed, supposing it to be administered twelve times a-year, though the assemblies might be less, yet might there not be about nine times more remembering the death of Christ, and nine times the force of prayer that now takes place on sacramental occasions? Nay, if these, in communicating work, should be strengthened as much in their inner man, as some have been by very frequent communicating, would not the force of all the prayers put up on sacramental occasions be at least eighteen times greater than it is at present? If this sacrament were administered every Sabbath, as we hope will be the case during the glory of the latter days, and perhaps sooner, what though the multitudes shall be less, yet are there not many more employed in the same work?[29]

But, indeed, if the meeting of a multitude be so necessary to the dispensation of this ordinance, why did not Christ invite all his followers (many of whom, we have reason to believe, were then in Jerusalem) to attend at his room to join in the first sacramental supper? If this room could not contain them, could he not have provided a larger one?

Again, does a multitude of ministers, with their various gifts, add any proper solemnity to this ordinance? Was the administration by Christ and his apostles less solemn

---

29. Brown references here the "glory of the latter days." Combined with statements from his book *A Brief Chronology of Redemption*, Brown seems to espouse a postmillennial view of eschatology: "But certainly, by the spread of the glorious Gospel, preached with the Holy Ghost sent down from heaven, all nations, Jews and Gentiles, shall be converted to Christ. . . . For a very long time, perhaps a thousand years' continuance, the Church of Christ in a most peaceful, pure, orderly, lively, and glorious form shall fill the whole earth" (quoted in Mackenzie, *John Brown of Haddington*, 176).

than ours, because there was but one minister employed in the administration? Was the administration less solemn in our covenanting periods, when one or two ministers were all the assistants? Has ever so much of God been seen at sacramental occasions, where there were many assistants, as where there have been few? Witness the sacrament at the kirk of Shots, and those in the north of Ireland about 1650, when compared with any sacrament where there were many ministers.[30]

Indeed, how can it be expected that the variety of ministers should add to the usefulness of the administration? Can there be any proper edification but according to the proportion of the divine preference? Is this divine presence always proportioned to the number of ministers? If it is not, might not people be as much profited though there were fewer ministers? What if endeavoring to please people with a vast variety of ministers, tends to encourage itching ears? What if God, like that eminent Assembly of 1695, count it robbery in ministers unnecessarily to leave their congregations vacant, especially if few or none of their hearers can attend in any other place? What if God count it robbery to deprive his people of the frequent use of this sacrament, by necessarily attending to assist others? If he do so, will not the presence of more ministers than are necessary be a hindrance in the way of the divine presence, and of proper edification? If God's power reach not the hearts of the hearers, what avails it how well their ears and fancies are pleased with the variety of ministers gifts?

---

30. In 1630, the small Scottish towns of Shotts and Stewarton became centers of a famous revival that centered on a celebration of the Lord's Supper. Similar revival movements also occurred in Northern Ireland at this time. See 11n16 above. For more on the background of these movements, see Westerkamp, *Triumph of the Laity*, ch. 1, esp. 26–28; Schmidt, *Holy Fairs*, 21–32.

I am not averse to the custom of a fast preparation, and a thanksgiving day, if the exercises on these days are considered as means for encouraging strangers to attend, AS THEY HAVE IT SO SELDOM AT HOME, and when they are considered as means for deepening the solemnity of the approach to God in this ordinance, which, in our present ease, is quite, or next to quite worn off, in the long intervals between ordinances of this nature. But is it not plain, that in case the church were returned to the primitive custom, there would be no need to encourage strangers to attend, because they would have weekly opportunities for partaking at home? And there would be less need to use means of this nature to fix or deepen these impressions; the conscientious approach to God in this solemn ordinance, the Sabbath before and the Sabbath after, would more effectually prepare the soul for receiving and riveting divine impressions, than all the work of these three days.

When these days [of spiritual] exercises are considered as well meant human helps, during the present unfrequency of administration, nobody regards them more than I do: but if anybody considers them, as too many ignorant people do, as essential parts of this ordinance, and plead the absolute necessity of them, as a reason against the more frequent administration of the supper, can I, in consistency with our Confession of Faith, chap. 21.1 refrain from detesting that view of them, and the usage proceeding therefrom, as REFINED POPERY?[31] Are they not of human invention?

31. The relevant text of the Assembly of 1645 reads:

> 7. That there be one sermon of preparation delivered in the ordinary place of publick worship upon the day immediatly preceding.
>
> 8. That before the serving of the tables there be only one sermon delivered to those who are to communicate, and that in the kirk where the service is to be performed. And

Was not the invention of them merely occasional? Are they not still unknown in many Protestant churches? Were they not unknown in the church of Scotland, for about seventy years after the Reformation? Do we not find one of our best Assemblies, namely, that of 1645, prohibiting to have any more than one sermon upon Saturday, and another upon Monday? Did not Mr. Livingston,[32] as long as he lived, refuse to allow any more sermons on the Saturday and Monday at his sacramental occasions? Now, is it not plainly Popish, to count human inventions, and occasional additions, *essential* parts of this great ordinance?

Besides, is it *reasonable* to plead the *necessity* of these exercises to the EXTRUSION of a divine ordinance? What would we think of the man who, when he had opportunity to hear sermons on Sabbath but twice in the year, had thought meet to appoint a fast-day in his family, a preparation day on Saturday, and the Monday for thanksgiving, on each of these occasions, if afterwards, when he might have sermon every Sabbath, he should refuse it, giving this as the reason, that he could not every week get three days set apart to the Lord, and that without this it would be a profanation to wait upon public worship, and the want of these would deprive him of all due impressions of this ordinance? The case is exactly parallel. Family worship approaches as near the solemnity of public hearing the word, and public

---

that in the same kirk there be one sermon of thanksgiving after the communion is ended.

(British History Online, "Acts of General Assembly," under "Acts: 1645: The Opinion of the Committee for keeping the greater Uniformitie in this Kirk, in the practice and observation of the Directory in some Points of Publick Worship")

32. John Livingstone, a Scottish minister involved in the revivals that took place in the 1600s in Northern Ireland and Scotland. See 11n16 above.

prayers, as hearing of sermons doth to that of communicating. Setting apart these three days for family worship on such occasions, is merely a human contrivance, and so also is the setting apart these days on sacramental occasions. Setting apart these three days for family devotion, in the above circumstances, might be very expedient, and may have the signal countenance of God. But could this man's three days of family devotion be lawful? Could it be blessed of God, if adhered to as a reason for neglecting to attend on public worship through the other Sabbaths of the year?

Again, if we look on these as essential appendages of the supper, why is it that we are not as careful for the reputation and credit of the sacrament of baptism? Why exalt we the one seal so far above the other? Or rather, why exalt we the one to the depression of the other? Is it not very awful to see professors come twenty or thirty miles to attend the sacrament of the supper, and yet, on the Monday, practically declare, that they think not baptism, the other seal of the covenant, worthy of a few minutes attendance?

In fine, whether it is grace or corruption that most affects to add human devices to God's worship, in order to make it more splendid than Christ has left it? May not persons be as really guilty of Popery, by doting on the splendid pomp of divine ordinances, that consists in the variety of days, sermons, and ministers, as by doting on the variety of fantastic ceremonies used in the Popish mass? Ought we not to beware of adding to God's ordinances, as well as of taking from them? Is God content to barter with us in this point, by giving up with the frequent administration of the supper, if we will annex a few more days, sermons, ministers, and people to it, when seldom administered? Where does he either make or declare his acceptance of this proposal?

Objection VI. Ministers could not endure the fatigue of visiting and examining their congregations between every sacrament, if it were frequently administered; neither could they bear the fatigue in their persons, nor the expense in their families; nor could the sessions support the weight of charges necessary on these occasions.[33]

Answer. What minister spends not too much of his time in trifling conversation, useless reading, or unnecessary sleep, etc.? Would he be at any loss if he redeemed that, and bestowed it upon the visitation and examination of his people? But if, during the intervals between the sacraments, this could not be accomplished, what law of God requires it as a duty? Did the apostles so? Do they all so who administer the sacrament only twice a year? Might not congregations be visited and examined as often as they are present, though the Lord's supper were more frequently administered? Might not the more ignorant, by frequent examination for some years, become more intelligent, and thus the work would become more easy? Might not many scandals be nipt in the bud, if the sacrament were frequently administered? Would not this relieve ministers of a part of their present troubles? Of what use, indeed, are ministers' bodies and spirits, but to be spent in

33. In my study of communion frequency in Reformed churches, one of my main conclusions was that the traditional Reformed emphasis on elder visitation before every communion made it nearly impossible to implement any of the Reformers' ideals about frequent communion. "Because the early Reformed communities, and those following in their wake, placed such a high priority on the mechanisms of church discipline, examination by elders, penance, self-examination, and preparation, these all tended to overshadow desires for frequent communion. In many cases, it was simply a matter of the time needed for all these activities. Hours, if not days, were required, and so patterns of monthly, quarterly, or even annual communion fit best within these structures" (Soderberg, *As Often as You Eat*, 255).

Christ's service? If they singly devote them to this, has not he promised, that as their days are so shall their strength be? Did not several of the apostles live to a good old age, notwithstanding their uncommon fatigue? If ministers, by an excessive care of their bodies, preserve their health and strength beyond the date of their usefulness, who gains by that? Are there more useless beings on earth than ministers in these circumstances? Besides, is not the present unfrequency of administrations the principal occasion of much fatigue on these occasions? Does it not tempt ministers to shift off their visitations, examination, and inquiries into scandals, upon the most trifling grounds, till there be a near prospect of another sacrament? Does not this bring upon them the whole load at once?

With respect to the expense in ministers' families, I would ask, what law of God or man requires that they should be at so much cost in their families upon such occasions? How much does it tend to the welfare of the souls of their family, or to the edification of others?

I would ask, with respect to the third part of the objection, when was there a sacramental occasion, when the collection was not more than sufficient to defray the charges? Will it not be found upon trial, that a penny for every communicant will defray the neat [*sic* = net] charges of the necessary bread and wine to be used in the sacrament? Will there not also be on every occasion something more collected for relief of the poor? Say not, there is a vast deal of charges necessary besides the neat charges of the elements? Are not these expenses, as to the most of them, rather *usual* than *necessary*? If sessions had to bestow them out of their own pockets, is it probable they would have made them so large as in some cases they are? Must these *unnecessary* though *usual* expenses in ministers' families, and upon sessions, be also considered as *essential* parts of this sacrament, the want of which must stop its frequency? Is it not evidently Popish to view these unnecessary charges as supports of the proper dignity of the ordinance? What would we think of the man, who thought fit to annex to every Sabbath which he observed, or to every diet of family worship, the preparing of a sumptuous feast, and the giving of a large sum to the poor, and then should tell us, he could not possibly celebrate more than one or two Sabbaths in the year, or observe any more than one or two diets of family worship, because his estate could not support the expenses he was put to on these occasions? Could this reason be sustained? Is not the application easy?

Objection VII. The Passover was administered but once a year; therefore the Lord's supper, which is come in its room, ought not to be administered more frequently.

Answer. Was the Passover a pattern for regulating the celebration of the supper by, or not? If it was, then, since nobody was required or allowed to eat the Passover more than once a year, does it not follow, that nobody is allowed to communicate more than once a year? Why then do we not warn our people of the sinfulness of communicating any oftener than once a year? If the Passover is to be our rule, why do we not attach also to the supper, seven days of unleavened bread? Besides, is the feast of the supper commemorative of the time of the deliverance, as the Passover was?[34] Why then is not the celebration of the supper fixed to Easter, the time when Christ was crucified? Are not Papists and Episcopalians exactly right in fixing the principal administration of it to that time? Again, was not the Passover to be eaten at the place where God's tabernacle or temple should be, and nowhere else? Why then do not

34. Exod 13:4, 10; 34:18.

objectors plead, that the sacrament of the supper should be administered only in one place, as Jerusalem, Rome; and that Christians should come up from all places thither? Indeed, in this case, once a year would be found more than many could attend. Besides, were women required of God to come up to the Passover? No.[35] Why then do we talk as if women were as much as men obliged to partake of the Lord's supper? In fine, did not the apostles know that the Passover was but once a-year administered? Surely. Why then did they administer the supper two and fifty times a-year, when they ought to have made the annual celebration of the Passover their pattern? Need I any farther expose the vanity of this objection?

Objection VIII. Frequent administration of this ordinance is a conforming to Independents.[36]

Answer. To whom do we conform in the unfrequent administration of this ordinance? Did not Papists first introduce the custom? Were they not the first who gave it a kind of judicial approbation, and that, too, at the Synod or Council which established Transubstantiation? To whom besides do we conform? Is it not to persecuting and bloody Episcopalians, and backsliding Presbyterians?[37] Are these

---

35. Exod 23:17; Deut 16:16.

36. Some of the Independent, or Congregationalist, churches practiced more frequent communion. See Soderberg, *As Often as You Eat*, 104–5; Davies, *Worship of English Puritans*, 204–16; Mayor, *Lord's Supper*.

37. Here, Brown refers to the history of conflict and persecution between Episcopalians and Presbyterians. In this context, "Episcopalian" refers to the Church of England and the Scottish Episcopal Church, both of which had strong ties to the English monarch. While the Scottish Presbyterians could be fiercely loyal to the English monarch—most Scottish Presbyterians were shocked when the English Puritans executed Charles I—they bitterly resented the repeated attempts of English kings and queens to impose the liturgy and

more worthy of imitation than the apostles, the primitive Christians, and all the Protestant churches at the Reformation? Must we refuse to imitate these, as far as possible, because some persons having great faults will walk with us a few steps? Besides, what connection is there between the principles of these persons, and the frequent administration of the Lord's supper? Whatever accidental connection there be, I challenge any man to show there is any in the nature of things.

Objection last. Mr. Boston, and other great men, never administered the supper more than once a-year.[38]

Answer. What if he thought the supper should be more frequently administered; but through the discouragements he met with from brethren on that point, or the prejudices he found in his congregation against it, deferred putting his sentiments in execution, as has been the case with many other great men?[39] How many have even sped from the press for the more frequent administration of this ordinance, who could never get their sentiments

---

episcopal church government of the English church on the Scottish.

38. Thomas Boston (1677–1732), a famous Scottish Puritan pastor, preacher, and theologian.

39. This was indeed the case. When Boston came to his first pastorate in Simprin, he found that the Lord's Supper had not been celebrated for many years, which was a common situation at the time in Scotland. So, he had to teach and prepare his people for coming even annually! Boston later pastored a church in Ettrick. According to De la Haye, "The communions were held twice yearly at Simprin, but only annually at Ettrick; even so, they were times of great refreshment, and a means by which the pastor could measure the progress of his people year by year. In each place, the numbers communicating steadily increased, to the total of seven hundred and seventy-seven in his final communion season in 1731" ("Thomas Boston," under "2. His Pastoral Method: The Lord's Supper"). For more on patterns of infrequent communion in Scotland see Soderberg, *As Often as You Eat*, 87–96; Burnet, *Holy Communion*.

reduced to practice? Indeed, what though Mr. Boston was of opinion that annual administration was sufficient? Are not the apostles, and many other great men among the ancients, together with Calvin, Luther, Owen, etc., nay, all the Protestant churches at home and abroad, particularly the church of Scotland in both her covenanting periods; our Books of Discipline; our Directory for Worship, etc., all against him in that point? What is Mr. Boston's authority, when laid in the balance with the authority of all these? Have not all the great men who have been of these sentiments, if indeed there have been any such, been ashamed of the public defense of their own sentiments, though they have got the highest provocation thereto from the opposite party? Ought we zealously to follow what they themselves seem ashamed to own?

> *Si quid melius nostri imperte*
> *Si non his utere.*[40]
> —Horace

THE END

---

40. "If (you have) something better (than) ours, share / If not use these." Thanks to Joseph Roberts for translation help.

Bibliography

Billings, J. Todd. *Remembrance, Communion, and Hope: Rediscovering the Gospel at the Lord's Table.* Grand Rapids: Eerdmans, 2018.

Bradshaw, Paul, ed. *The New Westminster Dictionary of Liturgy & Worship.* Louisville: Westminster John Knox, 2002.

British History Online. "Acts of the General Assembly of the Church of Scotland 1638–1842." BHO, n.d. https://www.british-history.ac.uk/church-scotland-records/acts/1638-1842.

Brown, John. *An Apology for the More Frequent Administration of the Lord's Supper: With Answers to the Objections Urged against It.* Edinburgh: Ritchie, 1804.

———. *The Systematic Theology of John Brown of Haddington.* Grand Rapids: Reformation Heritage, 2002.

Brown, William, ed. *The Life of John Brown, with Select Writings.* Edinburgh: Banner of Truth Trust, 2004.

Burnet, George B. *The Holy Communion in the Reformed Church of Scotland, 1560–1960.* Edinburgh: Oliver and Boyd, 1960.

Calvin, John. *The Institutes of the Christian Religion.* Edited by John T. McNeill. Translated by Ford Lewis Battles. 2 vols. Library of Christian Classics. Philadelphia: Westminster, 1960.

Chrysostom, John. *Homilies on Ephesians.* In *The Nicene and Post-Nicene Fathers*, ser. 1, edited by Philip Schaff, 13:49–172. Repr., Peabody, MA: Hendrickson, 1999.

Davies, Horton. *The Worship of the English Puritans.* Morgan, PA: Soli Deo Gloria, 1997.

De la Haye, J. R. "Thomas Boston: At the Borders of Glory." Christian Library, 1999. From *The Banner of Truth.* https://www.christianstudylibrary.org/article/thomas-boston-borders-glory.

Dougherty, Joseph. *From Altar-Throne to Table: The Campaign for Frequent Holy Communion in the Catholic Church*. ATLA Monograph Series 50. Lanham, MD: Scarecrow, 2010.

Gribben, Crawford. *John Owen and English Puritanism: Experiences of Defeat*. Oxford Studies in Historical Theology. New York: Oxford University Press, 2016.

Lewis, C. S. *God in the Dock: Essays on Theology and Ethics*. Repr., Grand Rapids: Eerdmans, 1970.

Mackenzie, Robert. *John Brown of Haddington*. London: Banner of Truth Trust, 1964.

Macleod, John. *Scottish Theology in Relation to Church History Since the Reformation*. Edinburgh: Banner of Truth, 2015.

Mayor, Stephen. *The Lord's Supper in Early English Dissent*. Eugene, OR: Wipf and Stock, 2016.

Owen, John. *The Works of John Owen*. 16 vols. Edited by William H. Goold. Repr., Edinburgh: Banner of Truth Trust, 1998.

Payne, Jon D. *John Owen on the Lord's Supper*. Edinburgh: Banner of Truth Trust, 2004.

Robertson, A. T. "John Brown of Haddington or Learning Greek without a Teacher." In *The Minister and His Greek New Testament*, 103–8. Repr., Vestavia Hills, AL: Solid Ground Christian, 2008.

Schmemann, Alexander. *The Eucharist: Sacrament of the Kingdom*. Translated by Paul Kachur. Crestwood, NY: St. Vladimir's Seminary Press, 1987.

Schmidt, Leigh Eric. *Holy Fairs: Scotland and the Making of American Revivalism*. 2nd ed. Grand Rapids: Eerdmans, 2001.

Soderberg, Gregory David. "Ancient Discipline and Pristine Doctrine: Appeals to Antiquity in the Developing Reformation." MA thesis, University of Pretoria, 2007. https://repository.up.ac.za/handle/2263/26414.

———. *As Often as You Eat This Bread: Communion Frequency in English, Scottish, and Early American Churches*. Reformed Historical Theology 74. Göttingen: Vandenhoek & Ruprecht, 2023.

Spurr, John. *The Post-Reformation: Religion, Politics and Society in Britain, 1603–1714*. Essex, Eng.: Pearson Education, 2006.

Stewart, Kenneth J. *In Search of Ancient Roots: The Christian Past and the Evangelical Identity Crisis*. Downer's Grove, IL: IVP Academic, 2017.

Taft, Robert A. "The Frequency of the Eucharist throughout History." In *Between Memory and Hope: Readings on the Liturgical Year*, edited by Maxwell Johnson, 77–96. Collegeville, MN: Liturgical, 2000.

BIBLIOGRAPHY

Tanner, Norman P., ed. *Decrees of the Ecumenical Councils*. 2 vols. London: Sheed & Ward, 1990.

Westerkamp, Marilyn J. *Triumph of the Laity: Scots-Irish Piety and the Great Awakening, 1625–1760*. New York: Oxford University Press, 1988.

Wieting, Kenneth W. *The Blessings of Weekly Communion*. Saint Louis: Concordia, 2006.

www.ingramcontent.com/pod-product-compliance
Lightning Source LLC
LaVergne TN
LVHW051711080426
835511LV00017B/2858